Copyright 2023 Crafty Turtle Talk LLC

Created by and for Crafty Turtle LLC. Characters created by Megan Craft and illustrated by Angelus Albarran. Backgrounds illustrated by Ishini Wijesinghe. Mission: Inclusion books, text, characters and illustrations Copyright 2023.

All rights reserved. Mission: Inclusion is a trademark of Crafty Turtle Talk LLC. No part of this publication may be reproduced, stored in a retrieval system, or transmitted in any form or by any means, electronic, mechanical, photocopy, recording or otherwise written permission of the publisher.

This is a work of fiction. Names, characters, places, activities and incidents are either the products of the author's imagination or used in a fictitious manner. Any resemblance to actual persons, living or dead, or actual events are purely coincidental.

ISBN: 979-8-9875109-2-6

Printed in the United States of America

MISSION: INCLUSION™
COLORING PAGES

CHARACTERS BY: MEGAN CRAFT, M.S., CCC-SLP

CHARACTERS ILLUSTRATED BY: ANGELUS ALBARRAN

BACKGROUNDS ILLUSTRATED BY: ISHINI WIJESINGHE

@mission._.inclusion1622

Copyright 2023 Crafty Turtle Talk LLC

MARGO

Copyright 2023 Crafty Turtle Talk LLC
@mission._.inclusion1622
www.mission-inclusion.myshopify.com

Copyright 2023 Crafty Turtle Talk LLC
@mission._.inclusion1622
www.mission-inclusion.myshopify.com

JASMINE

Copyright 2023 Crafty Turtle Talk LLC
@mission._.inclusion1622
www.mission-inclusion.myshopify.com

JASPER

Copyright 2023 Crafty Turtle Talk LLC
@mission._.inclusion1622
www.mission-inclusion.myshopify.com

LEVI

Copyright 2023 Crafty Turtle Talk LLC
@mission._.inclusion1622
www.mission-inclusion.myshopify.com

KEELY

Copyright 2023 Crafty Turtle Talk LLC
@mission._.inclusion1622
www.mission-inclusion.myshopify.com

NASH

Copyright 2023 Crafty Turtle Talk LLC
@mission._.inclusion1622
www.mission-inclusion.myshopify.com

ZOO

Coffee
Shop

@mission._.inclusion1622

Copyright 2023 Crafty Turtle Talk LLC

@mission._.inclusion1622

Copyright 2023 Crafty Turtle Talk LLC

@mission._.inclusion1622

Copyright 2023 Crafty Turtle Talk LLC

www.ingramcontent.com/pod-product-compliance
Lightning Source LLC
Chambersburg PA
CBHW080245121125
35326CB00059B/2582